LOVE

YOURSELF

PAY

YOURSELF FIRST

Dr. Abib Olamitoye

CONTENTS

FOREWORD

*The only bridge i've ever burned along this legacy i
dance is the one that linked the cities of prosperity
and chance.*

- Aesop Rock

I grew up under the tutelage of very shrewd parents who taught me
right from the beginning that to eat with one's ten fingers was the
surest and fastest way to remain eternally in the shackles of poverty.
I learnt the culture of saving right from childhood and that value
which I acquired as a young, innocent child is what has helped me
grow into who I am today.

True prosperity never just happens to anyone; it is never a matter of
chance. You have to make a conscious decision to be prosperous and
work assiduously towards it. The only key that can unlock the
store rooms of endless wealth for any mortal being is 'saving.' He
can never prosper, who eats all the seed of his harvest, not saving
any for the next planting season.

In this book, Dr. Abib Olamitoye, a living proof of the wisdom of
having a saving-culture explores the concept of 'saving' or 'paying
yourself first' as he calls it. The book is written in a simple, easy to
understand form that will appeal to a wide gamut of readers, while
driving home his points very succinctly.

I must say, Dr. Olamitoye is more than qualified to write a book that
teaches savings as the way to prosperity, as he has managed to build
and grow a vast empire for himself, using the principles he has
enunciated in this book.

I urge you to take that bold step and take a decision to improve your life; make today the day you start taking control of your money and your life! Buying and reading this book is the first step you need to take in order to gain that control and turn your fortune around.

Chief (Mrs.) Florence Ajimobi

First Lady of Oyo State, Nigeria

PREFACE

I congratulate you for getting a copy of this book.

Andre Gide once wrote that; "Everything that needs to be said has already been said. But since no one was listening, everything must be said again."

This, to me, is both funny and correct. Also true is this; the principle of frugality, saving, prosperity or wealth creation is as it is today as it was at the origin of time. It is the same, but the language of impactful presentation, the style of effective communication is different with each generation. Everything must, therefore, be said again in every generation. This book, Love yourself; pay yourself first, is consequently a modern tool, a new age compilation of the basic principles of true prosperity.

Far too many people have far too little of this thing called money. The study of the biography of mega millionaires and great billionaires revealed this fact: everyone who has risen and matriculated from poverty to opulence has discovered and employed this ancient principle of frugality.

Paying yourself first is the starting point, the core skill, in the accumulation of wealth. It is here presented to meet the challenges and taste of our generation. It is reader friendly, practical and entertaining. It comes in sixteen short, exciting chapters.

There is a race into which we are all preregistered. Every intelligent adult must grow up to partake. This is the agelong pursuit of fame and fortune. The man that will advance must begin by liberating himself from the shackles of poverty. All others must necessarily watch and worship, with envy and admiration.

Prosperity is good, empowering and preferable. Poverty is harsh and punitive. It is unnecessary, inexcusable and escapable. Poverty is a vice that must be hated by all men.

Now, two main bolts, if sufficiently addressed and released will readily pave way to freedom from poverty. The first is adequate self love. And the second; a flaming desire to prosper. If these two will be sufficiently addressed, all the remaining chains can be readily broken, and the annoying shackles can be easily brushed aside. Today, finally, you have discovered the manual that spells the manner of escape. About this, I must congratulate you.

While wishing you the best of luck, let me remind you that victory comes with application. Little application, little victory; no application, no victory; total application, then a total escape into freedom, abundance and opulence.

I welcome you to the hour of your grace; the moment of your glory.

Sincerely yours.

Dr. Abib Olamitoye Catford, London, UK May 2013

ACKNOWLEDGMENT

"Oh Lord that lend me life,

lend me a heart replete with gratitude."

-William Shakespeare

Let me thank the Almighty God for the gift of life, the priviledge of this message, and in anticipation of making the readers profit from the money, time and passion they will invest in reading this book.

The idea of writing a book on saving, as a core skill in creating a life of abundance, emanated from Dr. Tayo Apampa. I stay indebted for his contribution and encouragement in our concerted effort to help drive home the last nail on the coffin of poverty. I thank all the members of 100/10 Academy for their ideas, love and support.

I am grateful to all the kind hearted people who have committed time and effort in making this message available and presentable. To this end, I appreciate Bibi Bunmi Apampa, Tokunbo DesMennu, Adetokunbo Alli-Ajetunmobi, Adedayo Temitope and many others I do not have the space to mention. God bless you all.

I want to particularly thank the First Lady of Oyo State, Nigeria, Chief Mrs. Florence Ajimobi, the Iya Aare Atunluse of Ibadan Land, who has undeniably been acclaimed as the most compassionate, most benevolent, and the most beautiful first lady in Nigeria. I treasure the brilliant light her wonderful forward has bestowed on this book. If you will read through this book, and come back to the forward, it will be then, and only then, that you will be able to appreciate her imperishable taste for clarity, brevity and truthfulness.

I appreciate the illustrative and exemplary approach in which this forward was knitted, and the positive impact such would have in the life of the fortunate readers. God bless the Ajimobis. God bless Oyo State.

I am grateful to God for granting me an amiable soul mate, Olubunmi Gbenuade, my best friend and loving wife, who has created, in my home, an early heaven. I thank my two teenagers, Oluwaseun and Opeyemi, for their love, and for always giving me "something" to be proud of.

Finally, I thank you, the reader, who now own a copy of this book. I hereby confirm that you have made the best choice. I, therefore, solemnly, wish you the very best in life.

I love you all, very dearly.

"Success is liking yourself,

Liking what you do,

and liking how you do it."

-Maya Angelou.

INTRODUCTION

"Paying attention to simple little things

that most men neglect makes a few men rich"

- Henry Ford

The late legend, Earl Nightingale, fondly referred to as the Dean of personal development, once related a story about a six year old boy who kept demanding total attention from his father. Here is the substance of it, in my own words.

"Look at my toy, Dad, look at my toy" the boy commanded, "It's moving by itself. Can you see the flashing lights? The tyres are climbing, the horn is blasting, it is moving like your car, I will carry you in it when it gets bigger; you and Mummy!"

The man smiled. He looked at the toy for a while, and then redirected his focus on the live football tournament on the television. In a final desperate attempt to secure his father's undivided concentration, the boy went over to the television set and switched it off!

Not knowing what next to do, the man looked at his little boy and then at his blank television. He pondered for a while, and then came up with a little trick. He walked over to the book shelf, picked up a magazine, opened the pages randomly and sighted a large map of the world. He ripped off the page, gripped a pair of scissors and sliced the page into a dozen different parts. "Look, my boy, take this celotape, put this map of the world together and show Daddy how smart you are."

He then sat happily to enjoy the rest of his football match. In less than five minutes, the boy returned with the paper perfectly knitted together in a manner rather too clever for someone so young. Surprised, the father enquired; "How on earth did you put the map of the world together so neatly and so quickly? Would you please tell Daddy?"

The boy replied excitedly; "Look daddy, look at the back of the page, there is a picture of a man there, all I did was to put the man together, and then the world was together." The father was stunned!

He offered what seemed like a passionate and endless hug, saying repeatedly; "Yes my boy, when the man is together, his world is together. If the man will be together, his world will be together."

It is the responsibility of every man to put his world together, to put orderliness, discipline and learning in place. To create great habit and make them stay. To establish a way to get better, everyday, in every way.

A key component of an organized life is to take charge of your finance. If a man will master money, he will master all the remaining success factors much readily. Discipline in one sphere of life is said to have positive influence on all other spheres as well.

Our major duty in life is to succeed; for each person to create a great life for himself, his family, his nation, and then to leave the world a better place. Our task is simple; to search for and employ tried, tested and proven techniques; to mold our lives towards the virtues and persons we admire; to learn more and earn more; to know more and grow more; to enjoy the process and anticipate the desired end; to get and to give, to do all of these relentlessly for as long as there is breath in us. This, to me, is the technique of an organized, purposeful life.

The principles of saving as enumerated here are certainly not new. They have been employed either deliberately or unknowingly from the dawn of history, by every person who has conquered poverty and has created conditions of abundance and prosperity. The rules are simple and worthy of pursuit. The price to pay is by far insignificant when compared to the promise, the reward of a rich, meaningful and happy life.

If you will read and act on the recommendations, your life will manifest immediate improvement in a matter of weeks. You will notice order, serenity and a feeling of emerging confidence. If you were poor, you would begin to feel a sense of worthiness and the hope of opulence. If already rich, you will get even richer and happier.

By far, the greatest finding, feeling and profit in this new found life will be the spirit of self reliance. At last, you discover that you have within you what it takes to shape your character and destiny; that you are dependent on no outside capricious circumstance. You can then see a bright future, and the rest, a matter of time.

As you read, take notes, think about your life in relation to each of the recommendations. See how every idea or story can profit you. Come up with a list of action steps, a to do list, and then begin to act on the list. This is the way; the best way to self-love, self-mastery and self-discovery.

Key Lessons From The Introduction

1. It is the responsibility of every man, and woman, to put his world together; to put orderliness, discipline and learning in place.

2. Your primary responsibility in life is to succeed. You must never expect anyone to abandon his own, and take charge of yours. You must sustain the grip.

3. Man must take total responsibility for his fortune, or misfortune. He must have no one to blame.

4. Financial success is a process of mind over matter; to employ the creative abilities to search and find an increasingly finer tool of appropriating a better life for yourself and your loved ones. This shall be your key strategy.

5. The ancient principles of frugality and success remain intact and unchangeable . Every ambitious man must re-discover it, and employ the tenets.

6. The spirit of self reliance is antecedent to every success story.

7. You are never paid for what you know but for what you do with what you know. As you read, come up with a list of action points, and then take the needed actions. Also, this is the difference between knowledge and wisdom. Knowledge: what you know. Wisdom: doing something with what you know.

"The greatest surprise of human evolution may be that the highest form of selfishness is selfishness."

- Robert Ornstein

CHAPTER ONE

LOVE YOURSELF FIRST

"He that falls in love with himself will have no rival."

-Benjamin Franklin

An important duty in life is to love: to love our neighbors, our nation and our creator. We are told to love our parents and friends. This way, we learn to share love.

Long before the capacity to share anything of value was the capacity and willingness to acquire. We can never share what we do not have. This is true of love and money as it is of knowledge and wisdom. You love yourself, and next, you love others.

This is the way it goes: if you cannot love yourself, if you possess no self love, like a sunction pump, the vacuum for love in you will nag for filling. This will cause you to seek love, acceptance and approval from others. True love, coming from outside shall need to locate a receptor in you in order to be appreciated and appropriated. If you lack such sample of self love, any love from outside, however deep, will avail very little; you keep needing, you keep yearning, you keep nagging. This is the reason, the real explanation, why no amount of love from anyone can make sense or satisfy you, unless, and until, you love yourself. This is the same reason why no other person can make you genuinely happy. The seed of these attributes are planted right inside of you, latent, waiting and willing to be discovered, treasured and grown.

Brian Tracy, a commanding authority in the field of personal development came up with a unique formula for developing self love that turns out to be deceptively simple, but profoundly powerful.

Here it is: You affirm and say, "I love myself, I love myself," as many times as possible per day. You can suspend further reading now, and then give it a go. Say, "I love myself" about 20 times, feel the love as much as you can, and find out how much your spirit has been lifted.

Tracy recommended that you perform this exercise everyday upon awakening in the morning, and shortly before you drop off to sleep at night. If you will stand in front of a mirror, and then tell whoever you see there how much you love and approve of the person, and you do this sincerely, everyday, you add power and conviction that ultimately yield accelerated result.

Here is the tragedy. Many people think, and even proclaim, that they love themselves but are stunned when it is proved that the exact opposite is closer to the answer.

In many instances, we are our number one enemies.

The love we refer to here is a verb, to love. It's not the noun. To love is to act the part. The feeling of it can only be tangible in the action. The man that truly loves himself, in this sense, is true to type.

If he grows up to find himself in poverty, he acts to rescue himself. He wakes up and gets up. He employs only the scientific tools, and takes only the intelligent steps. He works hard to uncover the way out of penury; he learns the principles and negotiates himself towards the path of personal progress. He keeps marching until he becomes wealthy. He embraces and romances personal development. He takes the pain and commits to tasks that seem difficult and inconvenient so long as it's just, and promises a glorious end. He keeps doing all of these for the sake of the love he has for himself.

This man would do anything for the 'self' he loves. He is determined not to let himself down, nor will he act to betray the himself. He does all he ought to do, and does such promptly. He never complains of difficult duties so long as it is taking the lovable self away from abject misery.

There is no other way. You must start off by being your best friend, and enjoying your own company. If you are not, becoming the best friend of anyone can never profit anyone.

To love, my friend, is to show proof, and to demonstrate that for the entire world to see. A man that will not read books, acquire the needed knowledge and skill of his trade, conduct efficient service in order to deserve his income, and better income, such a man cannot qualify as possessing genuine self love. He is, in reality, standing in the way of his own success. He is said to enroll in the ranks of his enemies. He prevents his own success by ignoring the principles of success and accomplishment. One of the cardinal manifestations of genuine self love is this: *Pay yourself first,* from every yield of labour.

The will to pay the price of prosperity in advance is a manifestation of genuine self love. The will to prosper is common place. Everyone has that. What is rare, what you must possess, is the will to prepare to prosper.

As we learn, we earn. As we learn to love self, we must necessarily learn to pay self. The rule of paying oneself at all, as I said, is simple and unchangeable; *Pay yourself first*. This is the only condition under which you can pay others genuinely. It is only by paying yourself first from every earning, over a long period, that such money eventually accumulates, grows and multiplies to grant you a higher capacity to pay anyone else, and everyone else. This is the goal of this book.

Let me reveal this: if you cannot pay yourself first, every form of charity you undertake will always elicit some form of discomfort or pain. You will never give with joy if you have no growing reserve. You will never live with genuine joy either. God, they say, loves only the cheerful giver. To receive bountifully, it is said that; you give cheerfully.

You will be in good cheer as you share. This is true only when you have a good reserve unshared. This you must know.

As you read, I suggest that you follow the steps as outlined. If you do, you will uncover the great truth: that prosperity and greatness only arrive when you work harder on yourself than you do on your job.

Key Lessons From Chapter One

1. You must learn to love yourself first, and then, learn to share some.

2. Love yourself, approve of yourself, and accept yourself the way you were created. You are unique. This is the only condition under which you can treasure love and approval from others.

3. Love and happiness are inside jobs. Only you can grant yourself genuine happiness.

4. Stand in front of the mirror, study the person you meet, recognize the person, calm down and tell the person; "I love you, I approve of you, I appreciate you." Mention your name as you address the person. Do this daily.

5. Be loyal to yourself. Do everything humanly possible to demonstrate the love you have for yourself. Learn to teach yourself to"Learn and earn."

6. Be your best friend, enjoy your company and; practice solitude.

7. Find ways to pay yourself first from each earning.

8. Pay the price of success in advance. Cultivate the will to prepare to prosper.

9. If you have no cash reserve, you derive pain, rather than gain from any system of charity you employ or deploy.

"The starting point of all achievements is desire. Keep this constantly in mind. Weak desires bring weak results, just as a small amount of fire makes a small amount of heat."

- Napoleon Hill.

CHAPTER TWO

THE GENESIS OF PROSPERITY

"Love does much, but money does all"

-French Proverb

This book is intended for beginners, those who carry the desire, and the will, to prosper who seek the quickest and the most enduring formula, the infallible and reliable route to the accumulation of riches. It will be particularly helpful to the youth who is yet to form the wrong habit and belief system about money and has not grown to incur the sad mistakes and cash worries we see in most adults. To create a better habit, and correct all such mistakes, you now hold a dependable tool.

The core principle in prosperity is the art and practice of saving. As an art, it is like carpentry, driving, surgery or public speaking; you gain mastery by learning the basic rules and then putting them into practice. In any worthy art, proficiency is never attained or sustained overnight. You tend to fall, make mistakes, relearn the theory in order to learn from the mistakes, picking yourself up gradually until you eventually become a superstar.

You sometimes find a fortunate child whose parents or guidance are experts in the game of saving. They lay down the needed rules and serve as role models for him to emulate. This is a very rare example but here is the fact: we are not born great savers. We all must take the lessons and undertake the training until proficiency is attained.

Saving is not a popular part of the school curriculum and it is rarely seen as the seed of prosperity. No one may prosper in life or succeed in any business until, and unless, he becomes good at saving.

This book will prove priceless to many small scale business men and women, who must put orderliness in their businesses and take control of opportunities for growth and expansion. We have people, in their millions, in paid employments, both in private and government institutions, who have always waited for fat capitals in order to start the big business of their dreams. This may be the book that will finally reveal the truth that they can begin to save a little from their current earning until they eventually have enough to start little, and then grow into a position of affluence and prominence.

Entrepreneurship must always be seen as thinking big and starting small and learning your way to the top. The smaller you start, the greater the available room for expansion, the stronger the desire to improve. The habit of continuous improvement, what Tom Peters called "the relentless pursuit of excellence," once established, is the needed lever that hauls you and your organization all the way to the zenith.

Young entrepreneurs may not need a large loan or gift money to start a business. What is vital is the skill of managing money and the knowledge of and passion for the trade they choose.

People have received money all their lives, and many cannot provide evidence of frugality. If they get more, in all probability, they will spend in the same old imprudent way. To grant them more is therefore to arrest the thinking part, the imagination and necessity needed to sustain self-reliance.

All being said, the good news about the art of saving is that it is a game. It is learnable, practicable, fun and profitable. Like all beneficial undertakings, it is hard and cumbersome at the onset. Everyone at the top had kept at it, applied himself until it became fun and easy, and thereafter, had taken complete advantage to live a life of abundance.

Key Lessons From Chapter Two

1. You will cultivate the desire and the will to prosper. Ambition is vital, if you will maximize your potential.

2. Saving is an art, like carpentry, surgery, typing and driving. Mastery is attained and sustained by learning and regular practice.

3. No one is born frugal. We all must acquire the habit.

4. The way to save is not part of the school curriculum. It is not known in many homes.

5. The ideal way to derive any business capital for whatever line of business is the practice of regular saving from each earning, and the gradual accumulation of business experience as you put the money away.

6. Business is all about thinking big and starting small. As it's said, *"You keep your eyes on the stars, and your feet on the ground."*

7. It is neither ideal nor natural to start big, then employ many people to do what you can't do, or what you won't do. You will create a humble beginning with the job you love. You roll the sleeves and soil your fingers. It is these petty, minor or manual tasks of the beginning that you must master. You will then begin to delegate such as you learn new and bigger skills which are in turn mastered and delegated. This is the only way you are ever permitted to grow in business. You grow people in order to grow the business. You start with one person, yourself.

"The illiterate of the 21st century will not be those who cannot read and write, but those who cannot learn, unlearn, and relearn."

- Alvin Toffler.

CHAPTER THREE

ALL LEARNERS ARE EARNERS

You must learn to save first and spend afterwards.

- John Poole

We are all born learners. We learn to open our eyes, control our neck, talk, walk until we learn other complicated systems of the educational system and the skills of livelihood. We keep learning for as long as we live. Similarly, we are born earners.

Our income may come daily, weekly, monthly, regularly or irregularly, but we do get money. It may arrive in the form of salary, wages, gifts, tips, commission or allowance but it's earning nevertheless. The money may come from parents, older adults, school, friends, employers, customers or the government. In the game of paying yourself first, in order to kick-start a saving scheme, money or income is needed.

In many cultures, the new born babies begin to earn from their first breath. Wise and caring parents allocate some "love money" for their newborn. Well-wishers arrive to give some token to the mother. Larger income shows up at the naming ceremony. Parents open savings account or some saving devices. Each time the child receives monetary gifts, it is transferred into the savings account. As he goes through life into childhood, adolescence and young adult, he gets introduced to the habit of keeping money away, delaying gratification, the habit which later helps him to treasure frugality and prudent handling of money.

The young child is trained to put away in his saving account a little portion of every cash gift he gets from older visitors or any money he gets from parents. This is certainly not to suggest that children should be molded into money mongers by begging strangers, visitors or picking up stray or lost money from the street. All these must be forbidden. Honest earning must be the corner stone, the foundation or the core rule with respect to the art and practice of saving or acquisition of wealth.

Let us now look at the income that derives from the services you render. There is a law, promulgated by Earl Nightingale that:

"the income you get depends on the demand for what you do, how well you do it, and the difficulty of replacing you."

This means that you can increase your income by a proper use of imagination. You can choose a trade or a career you consider to be in high demand or lucrative and you perform such it an excellent manner in a way no other person can match. This being said, the general rule remains the same: the more you learn, the more you earn.

In the game of earning, one of the most insightful of all secrets is this: it is not how much you earn that matters, it is how much you keep.

Whatever your income turns out to be in any given month, the entire income is, in simple mathematics, 100% of your entire earning for that month. It is suggested that you apportion such into 10%, 10% and 80%. You then disburse each portion into different channels.

i. The First 10%

This is the portion you will save. The teaching is for you to put this saving away before you touch the remaining two portions. It is also recommended that you allow this first 10% to move into a separate savings account automatically; it no longer remains in the same account as the other two portions.

Further transfer should then be made automatic. You give the bank a standing order. It is moved by direct debit before you get the chance to see it. This is the process described as paying yourself first.

ii. The Second 10%

Franklin Delano Roosevelt once said that;

"The test of our progress is not whether we add more to the abundance of those who have much, it is whether we provide enough for those who have too little."

We make progress, tangible advancement, as we learn to share. It is on this premise that a tenth, the second 10% of our earning, is devoted to caring for the poor.

Giving away this tithe is beneficial. The more you give, as it is said, the more you get. The important thing to note is this; the giving should also be made automatic. You do this either by a series of post dated cheques or by direct debit mandate. This is as much as we can accommodate about this portion. Our chief concern, in this book, is the first 10%.

Key Lessons From Chapter Three

1. A major component of growth and development is knowledge.

2. We started off in life by learning to breath. We matriculated from laboured breathing to reflect automatic breathing. Here is the rule: we must keep learning until we stop breathing.

3. As we learn, we earn.

4. The first income is called "love money." Such love money should be saved by the parents.

5. As we go through life into adulthood, we learn to progressively refuse further love money. We then learn to earn every income. We take total responsibility for the flow of money into our lives. Love money is harmful to adults.

6. Only honest earning, the types you have worked for, endures.

7. To earn more money, take these three steps simultaneously.

    i. Create and improve the demand for what you do.

    ii. Conduct your services in an excellent manner.

    iii. Let your product or service be second to none.

8. The first portion, 10% of your income, is put away consistently and relentlessly.

9. The portion that makes you wealthy, from all the money you receive, is the part you put away, and never spend.

10. The second 10% is shared. This portion is donated to charity. The more you show fidelity to this structured benevolence, the more money, happiness and health you will attract into your life.

"I can explain it to you,

but I can't understand it for you."

- Unknown

CHAPTER FOUR

LOVE MONEY

"You have willpower, and if you use it, you will get your share of the luxuries of life. So use it to claim your own. Don't depend on anyone else to help you. We have to fight our own battles. All the world love fighter, while the coward is despised by all. "

-Theron Q. Dumont.

The pocket money, school fees, books, clothing, shelter, transportation and childhood expenses all require funding. The money comes from parents in the form of love money.

Let us talk a little bit about love money. Like the mother's breast milk, it is offered naturally and out of absolute necessity. It is beneficial at this stage of life. Love money is provided because parents and "adults" love you, and because you have not yet developed the skill and capacity to earn.

You derive love money throughout childhood until you leave school and join the labour market where you must render services for every cent you earn. This money that comes out of the "sweat of your brow" is the genuine income.

In every reasonable setting, the day you begin to earn from the labour market is the very moment you must give up the desire or longing for love money. Like the mother's breast, you must let go.

Love money is harmful to the psyche of every adult. It poisons the drive, pride and imagination. It destroys the necessity to focus absolutely on the yield of personal labour which carries the potential for unlimited growth.

Every young adult must learn to refuse love money. This is the only condition under which he can attain and sustain the degree of self reliance that is a prerequisite for financial independence and true fulfillment.

Here is another danger every adult must foresee, and why he must resist any temptation to dwell on love money. Love money is neither regular nor dependable. You have no control as to the arrival time or the amount. If it does not arrive quickly enough or it does not come in the anticipated quantity, you switch to negative mode. You blame, complain and develop hatred or bitterness towards a party that had been benevolent to you. This bitterness worsens if the money fails to arrive. All these prevent you from facing the stack reality about your financial life; that you must escape self deceit and, take total responsibility for your fortune, or its opposite; that if it's going to be, it must be up to you.

With longing for love money, your attention is distracted. You put less than your maximum concentration on the possibilities and opportunities latent in the career you have chosen.

The creative mode is enabled the very moment you bid a final bye to the idea of seeking, sourcing or anticipating love money. Suddenly, you are in charge. You are together, and pretty soon, your world begins to connect together. You must be willing, and ready, to say NO, with thanks, should parents and guardians persist in hauling love money at you. You will take to your heels.

Nothing can grant you the freedom, confidence and fulfillment that self-generated income will provide. Only the money you work for, in the final analysis, can endure.

Key Lessons From Chapter Four

1. All baby and childhood income, money spent during child rearing until a child begins to earn money by himself is said to constitute love money. Parents and guardians provide love money.

2. Love money is a component of parental role that must be withdrawn from all adults that carry the capacity to earn; this way, such an adult rises to take charge of his life. He assumes total responsibility and thus becomes responsible.

3. Every young adult must learn, or be taught, to refuse love money.

4. Love money poisons creativity, imagination and makes the man dependent, instead of being self reliant.

5. Addiction to love money, or longing for such, will keep the man in bondage to the source, and make the man negative and bitter if request for perpetuation of baby money is denied.

6. Financial freedom only comes to him that carries the desire and the will to earn every cent that flows into his life.

"There is no use whatever trying to help people who do not help themselves.
You cannot push anyone up a ladder unless he be willing to climb himself."

-Andrew Carnegie

CHAPTER FIVE

FREE MONEY

"He that would have fruit must climb the tree."

- Thomas Fuller

Many times, we witness the arrival of certain unsolicited free money in our lives or among others. Unlike the addictive baby money, this type can be tremendously beneficial and rewarding if judiciously invested, or if we carry the skill to handle such amount of money. Examples of this include inherited cash, property and businesses.

A child that will profit from inheritance is commonly prepared for such. All others will necessarily be ruined by the inheritance. The rule is to prepare the child for the business rather than to prepare the business for the child: to train the child, long before the arrival of the property and the money. *"Fortune doesn't change a man,"* said the Chinese proverb, *"it only unmasks him."*

Many adults seek "soft loan" from rich relations in order to begin a business. Here again, this approach can either help or hurt. Success will follow only if the adult is proficient at handling such money or business. It is never the business or the money that matters. It is the man.

E.S. Kinnear mentioned that;

"If you cannot make money from one dollar, if you do not coax one dollar to work hard for you, you won't know how to make money out of one thousand dollars."

One can readily confirm competence by observing how a person has handled money in the past and the level of business experience, passion and the will to learn and grow which he demonstrates. A critical test is to demand that he produces pain-money.

What is pain-money? This is the money he has put together, all by himself, that will be added to the loan in order to start the business. It is called pain-money because the loss of this money will cause him some pain if the business fails. If he has no pain-money to show, then `all he is` demanding is cheap money from you in order to experiment his proficiency in starting and running a business. If such a business fails, like it commonly does, all that will perish will belong to you. He walks away, a free man.

The point to note is this: the money he puts together, the pain money, will never be there if he lacks the discipline to save. It is this discipline that will be carried over to bear on any additional income that comes, as love money, from rich uncles, inheritance or the bank.

Key Lessons From Chapter Five

1. A child that will profit from inheritance must be prepared for such.

2. Parents who created businesses and wealth should train the successors, the children, the rules and skills of business and wealth management such that they continue where such parents stop. This is the ideal way to build and perpetuate business empires.

3. If parents cannot transfer the skill before they transfer the wealth, such wealth will serve to ruin the beneficiaries.

4. The will to seek money to start a business must be matched by the will to seek "knowledge first and application next." Money must be seen as a component of such application.

5. Handling a small business well, prudence in managing small money, is a pointer to a capacity to handle larger sums and bigger opportunities.

6. Banks commonly require pain-money: that which you have put together, all by yourself, in order that you benefit from soft loans to improve the business.

"The purpose of life, after all, is to live it, to taste, experience to the utmost, to reach out eagerly and without fear of newer and richer experience."

- Eleanor Roosevelt

CHAPTER SIX

THE PART TO SPEND

A man who both spends and saves money is the happiest man, because he has both enjoyments.

- Samuel Johnson

This is the third portion of 80% that carries the lion share, that part considered as available fund for routine livelihood. For many, this is the only purpose for which money is there to serve. It is the judicious use of this portion that makes continuous saving and charity program tolerable.

We live in a world where we enjoy the services rendered by others. Since it is mandatory that we pay for these services, we have a duty to set priority on our need, to put a measure, as it were, on wants and desires and enjoy only such services that will keep our expenditure within 80%, of our total income. To enjoy more services than the 80% can pay for is to take away from the first two portions, or worse still, to incur indebtedness. This is the cause of most systems of financial crisis. This is what we must work to guard against.

The other side of the coin is the key to prosperity; that is, to consistently and progressively spend less than 80% of the entire earning such that more unspent money goes back to swell the first portion of 10%, the saving scheme.

The services we enjoy come under several categories. These include all the shopping we do, the houses and cars we buy, the pleasure trips and holidays we pay for and other vital necessities like children's school fees, government taxes, utility bills and family upkeep. The list can be endless.

The provider or manufacturers of these items part with them in exchange for our money in order that they too can safely manage their own resources with the same orderliness as we have conducted ours. They pay their staff members, do some savings and charity, and some of their staffers come back to enjoy and pay for our own services. This is as it should be, if the society were to be in ideal setting.

The main skill of putting order on our finances is to find a way to contract the list of wants, prioritize the needs and delay gratification, such that our savings can profit from the unspent fund. We put limit on our wants and progressively drive the percentage of spending from 80 to 70, 60, 40 and so on. This way, we keep upgrading the first portion of 10% so it is reviewed upward to 15%, 20%, 30%, 40% and so on. It is by so doing and by investing wisely, that we can accelerate our march towards financial freedom. When we deliberately and intelligently order our finance, we bring meaning, organization and purpose into our lives.

Key Lessons From Chapter Six

1. The 80% portion is spent on the basic necessities of life, as well as to provide luxuries and gratification.

2. All our wants must be tailored to be in keeping with what the 80% can buy. We learn to set priority and buy only what we need and not necessarily all we want.

3. We find ways to progressively limit the amount of the 80% we spend so that the left over can be transferred to our savings, the first portion of 10%.

4. It is by the process of delaying gratification that we learn to deny needless wants.

"It is not enough to take steps which may some day lead to a goal; each step must be itself a goal and a step likewise."

- Johann Wolfgang Von Goethe.

CHAPTER SEVEN

SETTING GOALS

*"The significance of a man is not in what he attains
but in what he longs to attain."*

- Kahlil Gibram

Success in any undertaking begins with goal;

We have seen that the money to be saved must necessarily come from your income. If you consider your earning unsatisfactory, if your income is not regular or adequate, your first step is to go into a quiet place with a pen and paper. You write down how much you want. This way, you negotiate with life for your own "slice of cake." This is goal setting, goal writing. Napoleon Hill suggested that you,

"Reduce your plan to writing. The moment you complete this, you will have definitely given concrete form to the intangible desire."

The key to goal setting is to employ your imagination to consider a much higher figure than you currently earn. You set no limit on yourself. You write the exact amount you want with feelings that come with the ownership of such a figure. You act as if you already possess it.

As you write, ask yourself; "how will possessing this amount of money make me feel?" It is much later that you begin to figure out the way and means of achieving the money. In every situation, where determination can be found, the way can be found.

In an ideal setting, you determine how much you want in the next three months, six months, nine months, one year, two years, three years, 5 years and then 10 years.

This grants orderliness and synchronicity. You may need to punch a calculator in order to come up with satisfactory figures that will be in keeping with the estimated range of periods.

If you currently earn a salary set no limit upon yourself. You must remember that money can come from other sources beyond your fixed salary. You will trust your creator to intervene and show the way and means of meeting your target. The fixed salary can also profit from increase, allowance, commission or some other additions. No condition, they say, is ever permanent.

If your proposed or set income cannot come from your current employment, a better job that offers better pay may emerge. You will therefore keep your faith high and your spirit lifted.

You will also set goals with respect to how much you want to save in three months, six months, nine months and so on until you arrive at the ten year figure.

Lastly, you set goals on how much you wish to give away, as charity. You conduct this with precisely the same alacrity as you have conducted both the earning and the savings.

A particular concept, advocated by Dr. Joe Vitale that I have found remarkably priceless is the notion of setting a goal as to how much you want to earn from unexpected sources. It is like leaning heavily on your creator to expose a wind of fortune in your direction. This must be seen as a valuable addition to your system of goal setting. It makes you think bigger and wider as it reminds you that the accomplishment of your goal is not entirely left to you, and that your creator will answer if only you will ask, that the door to fortune may not open if you refrain from knocking. Like it is said, "If you do not ask, the answer is always no."

In setting both the income goal, plus the goal for the portions to save and share, you always ensure that each successive month manifests an upgrade. You always want to imagine more. To prosper, ambition is paramount.

All manner of goal setting and goal achieving, in the final analysis, is nothing more than applied imagination. Rather than merely adding figures, you must continually visualize a gradual increase in your revenue in successive months. You keep raising the bar on yourself.

The point to note about this system of goal setting is this: victory in financial accumulation is a matter of mind over matter; it is convincing your mind about the possibilities, it is applying faith and eradicating negative belief. You must also note that it is in the realm of solitude, spending time with yourself to jot down what you want, to visualize such, that will invariably lead you to the best way of manifesting such. You need a quiet time on a regular basis to keep yourself on track. Arthur Schopenhauer wrote this;

"He who does not enjoy solitude will not love freedom."

Key Lessons From Chapter Seven

1. Success is goals, everything else is secondary. Goals must be written with a deep and sustained thought as to how the accomplishment will make you feel. You dwell continuously on how you will feel when the goal is realized. Zig Ziglar said,

   "If you want to reach a goal, you must 'see the reaching' in your own mind before you actually arrive at your goal."

2. First, you establish what you currently earn, that is, adult income, not baby or love money. You then go ahead to determine how much you want to earn within a given period, and lastly, you dedicate yourself to its attainment with a singleness of purpose. You do the plan; you work the plan.

3. Goal setting is a process of diverting one's scattered forces towards a single desired end.

4. You must not permit the thought of a fixed income, a s in a rigid salary, to limit your drive to set higher goals.

5. You set goals on how much you want to save from your proposed income and how much you want to contribute to charity.

6. You also set goals on how much you want to receive from unexpected sources.

7. Imagination and visualization are the key tools for goal setting and goal attainment.

8. You must not bargain with life for pennies. In setting goals, your ambition should be high. You set big goals that carry the capacity to excite you. Christian Nevell Bovee was quoted as saying that,

   "We trifle when we assign limits to our desires, since nature hath set none."

9. Arriving at your goal should be the starting point of yet a higher goal. Aldous Huxley concurred when he wrote that,

"Every ceiling, when reached, becomes a floor, upon which one walks as a matter of course and prescriptive right."

"You were born to make manifest the glory of God that is within you. It's not just in some of us; it's in everyone.

And as you let your own light shine, you unconsciously give other people permission to do the same. As you are liberated from your own fears, your presence automatically liberates others."

- Nelson Mandela

CHAPTER EIGHT

THE DESTINY OF PROSPERITY

"Because your own strength is unequal to the task, do not assume that it is beyond the powers of man: But if anything is within the powers and province of man, believe that it is within your own compass also."

- Marcus Aurelius Antoninus

The point of learning about the art of saving is to cultivate the habit. This way, we master the art we save automatically, and step up to stay on top of our finance. This is the condition that invariably qualifies us to enjoy a life of wealth and abundance.

Now, how is this habit formed? With you, this far, you have engaged yourself with the idea of saving: the thought of paying yourself first, of crashing the 80% portion to free more money and generate higher savings deposits.

Now, why do you need to save? What promise does that hold? What is the purpose? Could it be the start of an investment that will be the foundation of a great career?

With the purpose clearly articulated, understood and admired, you begin to take some action steps, which in turn lead to further actions. It is this series of repeated positive and proactive steps that grow to form the habit. If you persist beyond this level, the habit becomes your character, an inseparable part of your being. It is this character that helps to direct and dictate further actions that lead you uncontrollably, inevitably, towards the destiny of prosperity.

Let me talk a little about the seed money. The figure 10% is not an absolute requirement to kick start the saving program. What you must establish is the saving habit: the day by day saving consciousness and the thought and act of frugality.

We have seen many prosperous men and women, who confessed to having started with as little as 1% which they had progressively upgraded to 2%, 5%, 10% and then up to as high as 40% or even 60%.

Here is the key: each time you think about money, think more about saving and less about spending. As it is said,

"What you dwell upon expands in your consciousness, and in your life."

You will prosper if you hold the thought of properity. Orison Swelt Marden said that,

"The creator has not yet given you a longing to do what you have no ability to do."

Key Lessons From Chapter Eight

1. The key to the art of saving is to get the habit.

2. You get the habit by taking repeated actions. You put away the first 10% of your income into a savings account and repeat this with every income for as long as you live.

3. If 10% is not convenient, you can start with as little as 1% of your income, and then improve on this as it becomes more tolerable.

4. Each time you think about money, think about saving, not about spending!

5. You never un-save what has been saved.

"A penny here, and a dollar there, placed at interest, goes on accumulating and in this way the desired result it attained."

- **P. T. Barnum**

CHAPTER NINE

THE POWER OF COMPOUND INTEREST

"The compound interest is the eighth natural wonder of the world and the most powerful thing I have ever encountered."

- Albert Einstein

The Compound Interest is the greatest money multiplier factor, and the greatest benefactor of those who practise regular savings. As you keep money called the principal, regular returns, the interest are added to your principal on a monthly basis. It is generally assumed that you loan your principal with your accrued interest to the bank which keeps trading with it. As you get further interest, the entire sum keeps rolling over to eventually become the kind of capital that can start a business or begin some form of investments.

This is how to make it grow even faster. As the principal and the accrued interests keep rolling over, you keep adding progressively higher amount until the combined sum becomes huge enough to cause an upgrade in further interest rate. The more the new capital and accrued interest, the higher the negotiated interest rate.

You can now see how the entire scenario looks very much like a game. It is indeed a game, a very profitable game, the kind that can ultimately make you conquer poverty and enlist in the rank of the wealthy; the kind that carries the capacity to generate whatever working capital you might need without recourse to a loan, begging or debt.

Key Lessons Chapter Nine

1. The compound interest is the greatest money multiplier factor, the strongest money magnet known, and the ideal route towards prosperity.

2. Your principal and the accrued interest when repeatedly rolled over, and then wisely invested, grant you the scepter of wealth.

3. You should allow successive deposits to manifest improvement. You cultivate upgrade consciousness. Always tell yourself that you can do better.

4. You can ultimately get any amount of working capital for whatever business you desire by trusting the compound interest, and sustaining your willingness to start small, as you think big.

"Nothing would contribute more to
make man wise than to have
always an enemy in his view"

CHAPTER TEN

KILLING THE ENEMIES OF YOUR SAVINGS

"There is no little enemy."

There is a war every man must win. As soon as he reaches the age of accountability, he must proclaim triumph over the vicious triad of ignorance, poverty and diseases. To accomplish this, only one strategy is necessary to attack ignorance!

Man must keep searching and keep learning about the pathway towards prosperity and great health. It is said that, "Health is wealth." The reverse is not so true. Wealth is not health. Man must therefore devote attention to the practical knowledge about the right way to appropriate salutary conditions.

The war over poverty is the subject matter of this book. Man must win little battles that stand in his way towards victory. This is the ideal mindset; it is vigilance; the constant and determined effort that breaks down the opposing armoury and sweeps away all obstacles. In a war, as in life, to be fore warned, is to be fore armed.

Like Sun Tsu said in *The Art of War,*

"To know them is to conquer;

to know them not is to be defeated"

Let us examine a few of these fierce enemies:

i. The Feather's Law.

This states that the moment you begin the process of saving, the entire condition and circumstances that will defeat your intentions will all arrive. They come, as it were, to subdue you, to beat you to submission and leave you defeated. You must bear this in mind, and take arms.

This situation occurs with savings as it does with all other worthwhile disciplines. If you make up your mind, for instance, to begin dieting in order to shed the excess fat, all sorts of dinner invitations will begin to arrive. All beginners in the discipline of saving also encounter similar barrier.

Ask any chain smoker and he will confess the number of times he had been defeated by free cigarette packets and gift matches soon after deciding to stop smoking.

The moment you set your first savings deposit aside, you come face to face with urgent and irresistible needs to spend the money elsewhere. Suddenly, your only sandal may dismember, or the engine of your car begins to need attention or your fridge may stop working, the house may start leaking or a close relative may threaten to die if you refuse to surrender your savings in order to pay her children's school fees. The list can be astonishing just as it can be endless. The thing to do is to save nevertheless. You elect to do the important, and delay, then deny, the urgent.

Dale Carnegie mentioned that you,

"Do the hard work first., The other jobs will take care of themselves."

The desire to save must be accompanied by the decision, determination and the discipline. These are called the 4d's of success.

If you stay committed to your saving commitment, one funny thing happens: the problem walk away, it solves itself, you become the victor. It thus, seems to me that nature repeatedly challenges you to prove your seriousness as prosperity is a "hall of fame" reserved only for the "Lion hearted." You get to be tested or initiated to confirm your worthiness.

ii. Impatience.

A number of get-rich-quick ideas and schemes line themselves up against you as you keep the savings pattern on track. Every rich person must overcome impatience in more ways than one. The urge to become wealthy over-night, like a thread, runs through the entire nature of the human race.

If we want to become slim and elegant, we want it now. The disease we have carried for five years, we want the cure in five minutes; the poverty that has ravaged our consciousness since birth, we desire its exit the next morning. As you begin to swell the file of your growing reserve, friends and relatives lay ambush to showcase ideas and deals that promise instant multiplication of your money. Apart from keeping your saving plans secret, patience, vigilance and prudence must all combine to carry you over this hurdle.

You never invest in a deal you have not thoroughly investigated or in a trade you are not competent at handling. The key is to beware, and to always seek the long term perspective.

You will find ways to ignore every doubtful opportunity in order to keep improving your reserve so you can take advantage of a higher grade, a more credible opportunity along the line. Opportunity to invest wisely will keep coming as you keep saving, and they will always match the range and capacity of your reserve at any given time.

iii. Procrastination

Procrastination is putting off actions or tasks to a later time. It is something we are familiar with. We all have delayed in starting or completing tasks or making important decisions.

Carrie Wilkerson wrote that,

"The longer you're not taking action, the more money you're losing."

You will, therefore, never delay the commencement of your saving plans. As you take immediate action, you derive motivation to continue. You will also profit from other sources of motivation and encouragement all the way through to the end.

He cannot truly claim to be wise who is putting off the initial step to salvaging his life from penury. All around us we see men in their millions, who literarlly languish in poverty, who postpone what they need to do, the seminars and books that spell the way to opulence and freedom. *"To get the power,"* as Emerson said, *"you do the thing."* You do it now. This money you now save will come back to safe you.

iv. Temptation

Subtle, irresistible and lustful suggestions keep ringing in your ears from time to time, urging you to spend a little from your savings. This must be interpreted to mean that you are being persuaded to transfer some portion of the growing 10% to the 80%. It shall also be seen as a case of misappropriation of your personal economy. The penalty for this is eternal penury.

Sure, you need to reward yourself or spoil yourself with each victory gained or with each target met. All such fund must derive from the 80%.

Why must you not nib a little of the growing reserve, occasionally, in order to celebrate yourself? If you do, you tend to arrest or halt the growing or expanding momentum of your savings, making you kick-start acceleration in the opposite direction. You have thus commenced yet another act, which invariably becomes the habit of depleting your reserve. As you take a little, pretty soon, you yield more easily to the temptation of yet another gratification until you wipe off every cent in the savings account. The sad part of this scenario is this; it is very hard to restart a savings scheme once you defeat your original plan or when you lose track of an established savings momentum.

Key Lessons From Chapter Ten

1. To become healthy, wealthy and wise, you begin by eradicating ignorance.

2. Paying yourself first as advocated in this book is the ideal way to triumph over poverty.

3. Many opposing conditions always stand in your w a y as you begin the process of saving. You must focus on your saving plans and ignore all such urgent distractions.

4. Saving is a lifelong process. The need to rush should be avoided. Patience must be the corner-stone.

5. You must investigate thoroughly before you invest your savings in any business venture.

6. You should only put your money in a business you are good at handling.

7. The more you save, the better and higher the quality of opportunity you eventually meet.

8. In starting to save, delay is dangerous. Your motto must be, "Start it now."

9. You must not yield to the temptation of spending a n y portion of your savings on items that will not come back to multiply the savings.

10. You must learn to delay gratification.

"It's in your moment of decision that your destiny is shaped."

-Anthony Robbins.

CHAPTER ELEVEN

THE COOPERATIVE AND THE CORPORATE THIEVES

"For what is the best choice, for each individual is the highest it is possible for him."

- Aristotle

Employees of a particular organization or members of a social club, for want of a common tie, sometimes embark on group savings and loan systems. In many settings, this is simply referred to as cooperative.

To further a common social interest, they enjoin one another to contribute a portion of their income into a special fund. They appoint money managers among themselves who later move the fund into a bank, either as an enterprise current account or as a term deposit account. Needy members are granted loans, in turn, with some interest charges.

This arrangement often grows so large and so complex as to exceed the level of competence of the handlers. The ensuing mathematical complication and manipulation commonly degenerate to undermine the safety of the deposit. Beyond the issue of skill and experience of the managers is this concern about leadership and value system; issues of integrity, honesty and transparency, not to mention that of vision or the mission. Cooperatives have no code of conduct and no independent supervisory authority of the kind we have with registered banks. It is the inevitable disintegration or collapse of the scheme, with the attendant loss of the entire savings that make victims label the cooperatives as corporate thieves.

The practice of socio-saving system, the cooperative, is obsolete in civilized societies, where money, the seed of prosperity, has since been elevated to a royal status; and where registered and credible banking system are available for every intelligent saver.

As you can see, putting ones income into any kind of cooperative cannot be a manifestation of wisdom, seriousness or self love. It is pretty much like plugging ones head into a dark and strange cave. Saving is a path to prosperity and greatness. Each person must tread the narrow, lonely path all by himself. You do not get rich as a member of a group of this nature. It is too social to be serious, too casual to be beneficial.

All banks are not alike in strength, reliability and corporate mission and value system. A few banks, especially in developing countries, are glorified cooperative savings and loans rackets of the types described here. Every zealous saver must therefore watch out!

Here is a general rule: the discipline and prudence of saving the money must match that of selecting the best bank to use. The safety of your deposit is by far more important than the interest it generates. It is safety first, and all other factors thereafter.

Key Lessons From Chapter Eleven

1. The best place to keep your savings is a registered banking institution. The second best is not good for you.

2. Your savings are important part of your life; therefore, its safety is of inordinate importance.

3. You will investigate before you decide on where to keep your money, and then choose the safest bank.

4. The cooperative is too risky to make it ideal for your savings.

5. The safety of your principal in your savings investment is more important than the promise of high interest rate.

"Those who save, have; those who have, get."

- Proverb

CHAPTER TWELVE

SAVING FOR THE RAINY DAYS

"There are two educations.

One should teach us how to make a living and the other how to live."

- John Adams

We can safely classify savings into two major categories. For ease of understanding this exciting game, we have savings for the rainy days, and savings for life. We deal with the first type in this chapter.

Saving for the rainy days, is the commonest type. The money to be so saved principally comes from the 80% portion, the spending part of your income.

As you have seen, you employ this bit for the provision of essential services rendered to you and your loved ones. Some of these services are minor and the money needed to procure them is meager, and can fall within the budget of your salary or income for the month. This may include the shopping for shoes, clothing, food items, cosmetics, bags, perfume, belts, toiletries and so on.

Depending on the nature and volume of your income, other items may be classified as capital intensive: Say the budget for a new home, a family car, landed property; even family holiday, school fees and marriage budgets may come under this category.

The savings you set aside from the 80% of your regular income to meet the demand for these "expensive" items is what constitutes saving for the rainy days. Discipline is needed in this area as in the case of the classical savings account.

What do you do when you need a new home? You open an account for it. You regularly put a portion of the 80% into this, and you keep doing so until it is big enough to match the price of the kind of house you desire. This is what you must always bear in mind; you will have one big project at a time, and you must sustain fidelity to this single project; come rain or sunshine. The German Proverb says

"The main thing is keeping the main thing the main thing."

Let me reveal a hidden secret about this concept of desire. Anything you desire becomes immediately jealous! Like the pretty bride, it stands to forbid rivals. You shall never, at the same time, want any other thing just as strongly. You will keep wanting the same thing until you get it. You concentrate the energy of desire towards this single thing you care about. This persistent focus turbo-charges you drive and thus accelerates the accomplishment of the thing you so desire. Sececa advised that,

"He who would arrive at the appointed end must follow a single road and not wander through many ways."

If what you desire is the latest model of the Toyota Prado Jeep, for instance, and you begin, you never spend such savings to conduct marriage or pay house rent since you have established that your major want for the time is the Jeep.

You must see that the point of these examples is to reveal the need to put some order and organization into your finance. Savings, in whatever form, grants the wonderful incentives of training character, focus, patience, concentration and tenacity in the person. This is the reason why it's often said that those who have not mastered the habit of saving cannot conduct a successful business. Saving is a skill that comes with all the habits of character needed to conduct a successful life as well.

The truth about saving for the rainy day, as they say, is that it seems to start raining much quicker than you speculate. The moment you set a goal to buy a new Toyota Land cruiser, and you open an account for it, is the very day you begin to see all types and models of the Jeep. It now appears to be more plentiful on the street now that your attention is focused on it. The more you sustain your intention, the finer your attention, and then, the closer you attract the jeep to your life. This is to mean that you eliminate all other competing desires until the original one is accomplished.

Key Lessons From Chapter Twelve

1. For practical purposes, savings may be classified as saving for life or saving for the rainy day.

2. Every savings you conduct, as a component of the 80%, the part to be spent, is called saving for the rainy day.

3. Examples of items that come under this category are such that you cannot buy from the income of one month. You therefore save regularly towards them.

4. You may need to save for a new home, a family car, some landed property, the family holiday and so on.

5. One important thing about the technique of saving for the rainy day is to have one capital project at a time. You set priority. You will then focus and avoid distractions.

"It is good to have an end to journey toward; but it is the journey that matters in the end."

- Ursula K. Le Guin

CHAPTER THIRTEEN

SAVING FOR LIFE

"The man who succeeds above his fellows is the one who early in life clearly discerns his object, and towards that object habitually directs his powers"

-Earl Nightingale

This is the second type of savings, the type which suggests that you pay yourself first. I am always reminded that this life is not a rehearsal for another one; that it is the real thing; and that it is worth living to the fullest. If this is so, then the best approach is to save towards a life of meaning and purpose; the kind you have always admired; the life of your dream.

Why do you keep paying yourself month in, and month out? Why must you love your life this much? What are the incentives and the promises? With regular savings come an uplift of your spirit; you manifest an upgrade in your self esteem, self image, self confidence, peace of mind and derive a sense of security.

Establishing a growing reserve is positive, it tends to attract more of its kind. The more you save, the more your capacity to save, the more money is attracted and available to be saved. The opposite of this phenomenon is also true; the more debt you incur, the deeper you sink into indebtedness. Debt, they say, breeds like toads. This is as far as we can say regarding this.

Let us continue with the positive. When will you experience the great feelings that come with saving? The moment you conquer procrastination and subdue the feather's law, and open your savings account, you derive a feeling of triumph. As you add more deposits, you keep feeling great. You will remember the saying, "What you feel about, you bring about." You invariably invite greatness into your life.

You will never encounter any collection of words that can accurately and completely describe the magnitude of hope, faith and promise that will come to the man who puts money away quietly, regularly and endlessly in order to invest wisely, and to construct the frame of greatness. It is when you begin, and persist that you keep feeling great, and attracting greatness. You then navigate the course of your life in the direction of your chosen destiny.

Let us look with an eye of pity at him who does not pay himself first, or who cannot do so. In his hand, you will see a long list of excuses as to why he must spend every cent that comes his way, and then borrow some.

Right at the top of his list will be items as not earning enough, or not even earning at all; having too many responsibilities that make the thought of saving rather cruel or unreasonable; having the yoke of loans to unburden; currently neck deep in debt; planning to start saving next summer; and so on.

Here is the secret; you start saving with as little as you can, and you stop further borrowing. You lay all the excuses aside and then resolve to give your savings plan the attention it deserves. The man who cannot save, or who would not save, is not safe. It is said that the gem of greatness is not in him.

Here is another secret. Learn your way to greatness. Your intention governs your attention. Put your heart on the subject of saving. Read the book, take the steps, form the habit, the character, and then, only then, will the destiny of prosperity and greatness manifest.

Here is a man we must examine clinically. He claims to have gained adequate mastery of the art of saving but his circumstance, environment and bank statements speak differently. The sight of him is sad. Something is missing; something is concealed. The will to learn is weak but the will to get is strong. Benjamin Franklin said;

"he who would not be counseled cannot be helped."

If help is to come, he must be taught the way to exercise self love to replace self deceit. He must learn how to learn.

The way to live in a fool's paradise, and millions do, is to pay the self first, then un-pay the self by spending the savings, come back to saving and then spend it, again and again, in a manner similar to taking one step forward and two steps backward. People mistake having a bank account with competence in the art of saving.

There are classically two classes of people since the dawn of civilization; the poor and the rich. The rich are said to typically pay themselves first, and then spend the rest; while the poor always spend first and then save the remaining. As you know, nothing ever remains. Now, which class do you prefer? It is always in the end that regret and frustration appear to him who employs the wrong tools.

Key Lessons Chapter Thirteen

1. Your life must be taken very seriously. A way to demonstrate the seriousness is to pay yourself first, and then, to keep doing so for as long as you breath.

2. The more you save, the more money is attracted to you, the higher your self-worth, self-image, self-confidence, and the more your feeling of competence.

3. Establishing a growing reserve grants hope and opportunities for advancement.

4. You must lay aside all excuses and take charge of your finance.

5. You must read books and keep reading great books about money and business. You must apply the knowledge so gained.

6. You must determine why you are saving, the purpose. What business or investment are you going to start with the saving? As you save, you keep this purpose in view, and never backslide.

"We may not achieve everything we dream, but we will not achieve anything unless we dream."

- Gurbaksh

CHAPTER FOURTEEN

HOW I SAVED FOR THE RAINY DAY

"Goals provide the energy source that powers our lives. One of the best ways we can get the most from the energy we have is to focus it. That is what goals can do for us; concentrate our energy."

- Denis Waitley.

Soon after leaving the university, as a medical doctor, in the fall of 1985, I needed a car very desperately. I proceeded to write it out as a goal; to own a car within the year of internship at the state hospital, Ijebu-Ode, Ogun State, Nigeria. It sometimes seems one only has to want a thing greatly to get it.

Besides *"Think and Grow Rich"* by Napoleon Hill, and *"How To Win Friends and Influence People"* by Dale Carnegie that led me into a life of perennial personal development, I had read two other great books about the principle of saving, back in my university days. They are: *"Instant Millionaire"* and the *"Richest Man in Babylon."*

This was to be the time to put all I had read into practice. On the surface, it was practically impossible for me to own a car within one year, given the amount of money we were paid as intern doctors at the time. I resolved to get a car nevertheless, leaning heavily on faith and a resolute determination.

I sat to analyze how much it would cost me to keep alive, go to work and pay my bills within one month. It became immediately evident that transportation alone would consume almost 60% of my income. I was then left with only one strategy, a single game plan. In order to get a car, I had to give up taxis. I had to get on my feet every morning, and evening, if my dream was to come true. The round trip was approximately ten miles.

I found it very challenging during the first few weeks. I had to wake up earlier than others, set on the street before everyone in order to arrive at the hospital about the same time as those who boarded taxis.

At the close of work in the evening, I had to dash pass the row of hospital workers who waited in turn to get taxis. I was always seen equipped with my famous umbrella. The news soon went round the hospital that the new doctor called Olamitoye never took taxis, always pounded the street to and from work, in rain or sunshine. It wasn't long before I acquired a nickname in this regard: Dr. Olurin, which literally meant "Dr. Land-cruiser."

A few times, some of the nurses and colleagues would wind down the windows of their taxis to yell the sound of "Land Cruiser" in some derogatory tones.

I once read that;

"A man of sense is never discouraged by difficulties, he redoubles his industry and his diligence, he perseveres and infallibly prevails at last."

I also got a few ridiculous comments from friends, some of who had cars bought for them by their rich parents. They referred to my mode of transportation as "foot-wagen" instead of the "Volkswagen" car they had.

Somehow, I learnt to live with all of these. I stayed determined to save every income, except for the feeding and upkeep allowance I granted myself. Wilfred Peterson counseled that:

"Success is focusing the full power of all you are on what you have a burning desire to achieve."

I read my two books on saving during the first week of every month, almost like a ritual, and that helped to keep the hope alive, to keep the fire burning, and to sustain the much needed focus and concentration.

Here is the fact: Desire is vital to accomplishment. Sheila Graham mentioned that,

"You can have anything you want if you want it desperately enough. You must want it with an exuberance that erupts through the skin and joins the energy that created the world."

I bought my first car, a second hand Datsun 180k, about nine months after I started my saving program. Again, news went around the hospital that Dr. Land-cruiser had bought a car. Congratulatory handshakes came from all and sundry. I'm sure it was Nikola Tesla who wrote that;

"I do not think there is any thrill that can go through the human heart like that felt by the inventor as he sees some creation of the brain unfolding to success. Such emotions make a man forget food, sleep, friends, love, everything."

The feeling that I had a car parked outside my residence granted me a delight I had never experienced. I lost the early morning rush, the mandatory evening walk and all the tag of ridicule forever. I felt grateful and compensated every time I saw the car.

I was to later help many of my "taxi-friendly colleagues" and friends who scorned by primitive mode of transportation during my land cruising days. They joined me in the Datsun car as I drove home and dropped them off at the junctions closest to their residences. Many of them confessed that they had to call me such names because my approach cheapened the status of a medical doctor. Some jokingly said that they thought I was possessed by the "demon" of miserliness. One mentioned that I took stinginess rather too far, that what he saw in me was a pathological case of excessive prudence. However, the victory was worth the pain in the end.

Let me leave you with this encouraging words from Charles Popplestone,

"You can really have everything you want, if you go after it, but you will have to want it. The desire for success must be so strong within you that it is the very breath of your life- your first thought when you awaken in the morning, your last thought when you go to bed at night."

Key Lessons From Chapter Fourteen

1. Desire is the starting point of all worthy accomplishment.

2. You must commit every desire to paper. You will then read books on how to acquire or accomplish the goals you have set.

3. Determination and discipline are important components of getting what you want.

4. Thorough preparation, doing your "homework" helps grant the needed approach and the winning formula.

5. Nothing worthwhile comes easily.

6. Friends and well-wishers, though well meaning, may sometimes throw discouraging attitudes and damaging comments on your path. You must, nevertheless, remain focused and stay on track.

7. Knowing why you want what you want helps to strengthen the will.

8. Victory is sweet and it is worth the effort.

"Only those willing to do what the very few do will get the rewards that the very few get."

- Robin Sharma

CHAPTER FIFTEEN

HOW I SAVED FOR LIFE

"The dream is not what you see in sleep;

Dream is the thing which doesn't let you sleep."

- Dr. Abdul Kalam

I drove my car around the town of Ijebu-Ode for another three months until the completion of my internship program. I was to begin another set of one-year program in National Youth Service Corps Scheme (NYSC). I was posted to Ejigbo in the then Old Oyo State of Nigeria.

The gains and experiences I got from the prudent handling of my income in Ijebu Ode inspired me to save even harder during my NYSC year. I wrote a goal to save enough money from the corper's allowance or salary in order to eventually begin a private hospital of my own. I always had this dream since my university days: to be on my own, to start a hospital and save myself the pain of searching for jobs, to be able to create jobs for others.

If I was to acquire any expertise or the skill of medical practice, it would have to come from my diligence and willingness in the year of internship. I did everything humanly possible to milk sufficient skills from our four consultants as we rotated round them on a quarterly basis. This was later proven priceless during my independence in private practice.

I perfected the skills in Ejigbo at the Comprehensive Health Centre where I served as the only registered medical doctor in government employment, in the entire local government at the time.

The strategy I employed was simple and similar to the one used during my internship year. Here, I saved all my NYSC allowance, and all doctor call-duty allowance and lived absolutely on the meager income I got working as a locum evening doctor at a private hospital in the town. The money I derived from this private arrangement was approximately 25% of my NYSC allowance. I got tremendous help from my landlord who permitted me to stay free in the house without paying rent. In exchange, I offered free medical attention to him and his entire large family.

I spent the NYSC year putting plans and procurements together that would enable me to start Tolu Medical Centre, my first private hospital, precisely three days after the NYSC passing out parade. I am tremendously grateful for the privilege and the ability to navigate my thought and action away from spending my income, so I could dwell and act more on saving and investing. This rare grace, from God, to me, made all the difference.

Key Lessons From Chapter Fifteen

1. As you learn to save, and put such knowledge to work, you get the needed experience to profit more from the skill.

2. You should find a way to stick to your dream until its realization.

3. As you earn and save money towards your career, you must learn and master the trade you intend to invest the money on.

4. It thus seems that when you finally make up your mind on a life journey to travel towards, and begin the trips, all unforseen help and mercies begin to aid your progress.

"Our first journey is to find that special place for us."

- Earl Nightingale

CHAPTER SIXTEEN

THE STRATEGY FOR PAYING YOURSELF FIRST

"In the family, as in the state, the best source of wealth is economy."

- Cicero

Here are the main points to note about saving for life.

1. Begin by determining the kind of investment, career or purpose into which you intend to employ the savings.

2. The investment must be the kind that will grow and multiply your savings and mature to yield one or more perenial streams of income.

3. You will set a goal in that direction. The goal shall be written and time bound.

4. You will determine how long it will take to accumulate the amount of money needed as the startup capital, the sum that will permit you to start small.

5. As you begin your savings program, you will also commence the process of gathering the knowledge, skill and experience that will be needed to excel in the career or investment you have identified.

6. You will stick, with steel tenacity, to your savings project as well as to the art and skill of starting, running and excelling in the trade you have chosen.

7. If you run a business, you must see the company as a separate entity. It shall have its own saving scheme in place. In the corporate world, this is called the "sinking fund." This money accumulates over a long time to permit the business to profit from expansion or to take advantage of bigger opportunities. It is said that a company that does not have a sinking fund in place would invariably sink. The company must also contribute to charity the same way as we have described for the individual.

8. Your mortgage, if you have one, is a component of your "rainy day" desires. As you redeem the payment, it is vital that you nurse a secret "saving for life." You do not live in order to pay the mortgage; the mortgage is there only to provide a place to live in. Everyone alive must find a purpose, save towards the purpose as he pursues the purpose. This is your profession. Vincent Van Gogh wrote,

"Your profession is not what brings home your pay check. Your profession is what you were put on earth to do, with such passion and such intensity that it becomes spiritual in calling."

9. If you catch yourself neck-deep in debt. Running away will not do. Take the following six action steps all at the same time.

   i Write the entire amount on paper and schedule repayment patterns, and keep to the plan.

   ii. Reduce your spending, and block all possible areas of waste.

   iii. Stop further borrowing; throw away the credit card.

   iv Begin to safe for life; keep a saving plan.

   v. Contribute to charity.

   vi. Find ways to increase your income..

10. This much you must remember: above all, save for life, forever living should be forever saving. You must bear in mind that those who save derive great hopes; and those who have hopes enjoy happiness, strength, serenity and longevity.

"Saving comes too late

when you get to the bottom."

- Seneca

CHAPTER SEVENTEEN

21 NUGGETS OF TRUTH ABOUT MONEY

"Spend not where you may save; spare not where you must spend."

- John Ray

1. Create a positive belief system about money. Money is good and important. It is just as wonderful as the comfort it will provide, the childhood education it will grant, the good homes, great environment, hospital bills and all other basic necessities, and luxury it will permit.

   Always believe that you carry the destiny of prosperity and conduct your thinking in this manner.

2. Desire to prosper. You will develop sufficient and increasing desire to prosper. Desire is the starting point, and the needed fuel that propels you onward in the direction of your dream.

3a. Think well and positively about all wealthy people . Never resent rich people! This way you repel wealth unconsciously. The great billionaires and mega-millionaires and all the well-to-do people of your environment should serve as mentors and role models. Find ways in your heart to associate love, admiration and positive feelings with all wealthy people. Never dwell on the short comings of wealthy people. They are humans. Think only about what you like in them.

b. Never join others to denigrate prosperous people. If you find yourself in a group where they speak ill of a rich person or where they link prosperous people with selfishness, slander and recklessness, save yourself the pain. Never join t h e m to perpetuate such. It will only serve to poison your soul. Find a way to walk away.

4. Set goals. Learn to set income goals, saving goals and charity goals. Think big as you do.

"Until you commit your goals to paper," a wise man once said, *"you have intentions that are seeds without soil."*

Here is a choice you have to contemplate; "If you bring a spoon to God, He will fill it. If you bring a bucket to God, He will fill it, If you bring 50-gallon barrel to God, He will fil that, too. Which best describes your expectation from God to fill a spoon, a bucket or a barrel?"

5. Love yourself. Above all, love yourself.

6. Pay the price of success in advance. The will to prosper is common place. Everyone has that. What is rare, and what you must have, is the will to prepare to prosper.

7. Pay yourself first. Make the payment automatic. Learn more about the skills of saving.

The key to financial success has always been: Pay yourself first! Put it away in a savings account for long term investment and never touch it for any reason. Your ability to save money is a measure of your character. It is a test of your self discipline and will power. It makes a bold statement about your basic values as a human being. "It is the law of God that unto him who keepeth and spendeth not a certain part of all his earnings shall gold come more easily."

8. Contribute to charity. Make it automatic as well. Learn about the great ways to give.

9a. Invest only in a business you care about, the business you love, the type that you would be glad to do free.

b. Never love an unprofitable business.

10. Always investigate before you invest. Consider the following:

a. The safety of your principal or capital.

b. Return on investment. The time it takes for the money you invest to return.

c. Opportunity cost. This is the alternative venture that would generate quicker, steadier and better return on your investment.

11. Organize your earning into a Pareto structure; 80/20 Law.

a. Spend 80%

b. Save 10%

c. Give 10%

To really prosper, take more from the spending portion to your saving account and keep improving on this everyday of your life.

12. There is power in prayer. Learn to take maximum advantage of this. Four steps to accelerated achievements, "Plan purposefully. Prepare **prayerfully.** Proceed **positively.** **Pursue** persistently."

13. Affirmation is a great weapon of achievement. Find ways to create positive affirmation about money, wealth and income. Here are my favorites.

a. Every day in every way, I am getting better and better.

b. All is well with my income and income sources.

c. I am getting richer and richer.

d. I like money. I love money. Money is constantly circulating in my life.

e. I release money with joy and thankfulness and it returns to me multiplied in a wonderful way.

f. I am a generous billionaire.

g. I use money for good only and I am grateful for my good and for the riches of my mind.

14. Health is wealth. Wealth is not health. Health grants energy, energy grants ideas, idea grants money. Find ways to eat well, exercise well and rest well.

15. Enjoy your life. Recreate. Take time off from routines. Recharge your creative batteries. It has been said that, "There are two things to aim at in life. The first is to get what you want. And after that, the second is to enjoy it. Only the wisest of mankind achieves the second."

16. Employ the power of emotion, feelings.

    a. Ask, how does it feel like to be a billionaire? Dwell more on this.

    b. Before you do anything, eat anything, stay anywhere, ask: Are these the kind of things billionaires do? If not, don't do it.

    c. Think like a billionaire. Have the awareness, and the consciousness; employ billionaire mentality every waking moment of your life.

17. Associate with advancement oriented, goal oriented people. Get away from losers. Give generously to the poor, help them, but don't enroll in their ranks. You cannot help the poor by becoming one of them.

18. Never allow amateurs, people without proven great track records, to trade with your money. Take business ideas and advice only from practical people; those you want to resemble.

19. Avoid debts, escape debt.

    a . If you must take a loan, generate a plan and means of repayment long before you touch the money. Follow the repayment pattern to the letter. Always sustain your integrity at all times.

    b. Get out of debt as fast as you can.

20. Follow your heart.

21. In your quest for money and all that money can buy. Never forget, or abandon, what money cannot buy; your self-love, the love of your family, your nation and your creator. *"A man's true wealth,"* said Bendix Line, *"the good he does in the world"*

CHAPTER EIGHTEEN

CONCLUSION

1. The Principle Of Prosperity

i. The words "principles of prosperity" refer to certain classified information that is known or shared by a very privileged few, the information that is acted upon by a tiny percentage of those who learn about it.

ii. It's the decided action taken by such minority on this vital information that makes only very few people very rich.

iii. It is the inability or unwillingness on the part of a great majority, close to a whopping 90% of the people, to gain access to this vital document, and to act promptly on the content, that is the complete explanation for the pandemic proportion of poverty.

2. Money Wisdom

2.1. There's such a thing as money wisdom. Those who possess this become rich.

2.2. A great desire to prosper is antecedent to all forms of financial attainment.

2.3. That which one man attains can be attained by any other man, provided he carries similar desire, and the path and principle remain the same.

2.4. You must never deride the principle of prosperity because of its simplicity. The synonym for principle is truth, and truth is always simple. Truth always sets him free that seeks and obeys it.

2.5. You must keep a savings account and transfer a minimum of 10% of whatever money you earn beginning from the time you know about this principle until your last day on earth. You must resist the temptation to spend a portion of it on anything that will not make it grow.

Money may come to you in the form of salary, profit, wages, bonus, commission, allowance, and gifts.

2.6. This principle, if followed, will invite others, and together, you shall be set free from the triplets of ignorance, poverty and disease.

2.7. A man that keeps money in this manner will develop money consciousness. To him who manifests money consciousness shall more money be added.

2.8. A man who does not obey the rule as spelt above shall have fear consciousness. Fear is the enemy of prosperity. Fear consciousness attracts poverty.

2.9. From him who keeps none, or has none, even the little he has shall be attracted to the person who saves money. Money moves to the area of high concentration of money. Money moves away from where it is scarce. Money attracts money! This is the law of attraction at work. This is the reason why the rich tend to get richer and the poor tend to get poorer.

2.10. The possession of money consciousness confers confidence. Confidence invites the feeling of competence. That which you feel about, you bring about. The acquired competence attracts the opportunity to earn more.

2.11. The truth or the application of the principle is the only known cure for fear. Many principles exist. They together serve to salvage man from the jaws of fear.

2.12. Ignorance of the principles is not permitted as excuse for disobeying the principles. The penalty shall be equally met.

2.13. You either choose the principle, the truth, and the freedom it brings, or by default, you live with the fear and the poverty and slavery they bring.

3. War Against Expenses.

3.1. You must control your expenses.

3.2. Expenses grow to meet income. If your income increases, your expenses will immediately rise to match the increase. You have a duty to resist the rise.

3.3. Uncontrolled expenses or unnecessary expenses are the enemy of prosperity.

3.4. Expenses, left to themselves, always multiply themselves.

3.5. Multiplication of expenses always multiplies stress and aggravates anxiety and fear.

3.6. Writing out the list of all possible expenses immediately brings them under control. The more you delete from the list, then the higher your feelings of victory over fear, and consequently, the greater your level of confidence. Whatever is deleted shall be added to the savings.

You will check to confirm what you buy every day, you will find out the top three items you spend money on, everyday. Such items are immediate suspects, and should be charged for standing in your way, for stalling your progress, and for aiding and abetting poverty. They shall be deemed guilty as charged until proven otherwise.

3.7. Impulsive buying is a known precipitator and accelerator of poverty.

3.8. Every expenditure should be scrutinized as to its real value to your life, especially in your quest towards wealth.

3.9. Expenses that cannot pass the value test must be resisted and the worth in monetary terms should be added to your savings.

4. Putting Money To Work

4.1. You must find ways to invest your savings.

4.2. In any form of investment, the very first step is thorough investigation.

4.3. The safety of your savings is more important than the flamboyant promise of a high yield of interest.

4.4. It's very true that the money you safe always suffer depreciation as a result of inflation of your currency. You will nevertheless go ahead and keep saving. Your growing reserve will fetch you incalculable confidence, compound interest, and attract more money to itself. All these benefits combine with your feeling of security and peace of mind to sink the thought of inflation into insignificance.

4.5. The money you save will come back to safe you.

4.6. A man who does not save, a man who cannot save, is not safe.

4.7. Always nourish a strong desire to invest your savings so that the money you work for will take over and begin to work for you.

4.8. The harder your money works by the speed of return on investment, or level of interest rate, the richer you become.

4.9. The higher the figure you regularly save, the faster you accelerate towards prosperity.

4.10. Nearly ninety nine percent of wisdom consists in being wise in time. The earlier you begin your saving program, the more your chances of early arrival at the hall of fame and fortune.

4.11. True wealth and peace of mind are second cousins just as fear and poverty are identical twins.

4.12. Dubious acquisition of wealth, on the long run, is a prescription for social disaster and humiliation.

4.13. You must beware of investing in the good idea of a very close ally or a family member who does not follow the principle. The man who does not save will not treasure the sacrifice and pain of delaying gratification. His advice and intervention may heighten the risk of losing your money.

4.14. The best investment for your money is the same industry where it has its origin.

4.15. The worst investment for your money is the industry you know very little or nothing about.

4.16. Investing in an industry you are not familiar with is a great multiplier of fear, confusion and stress. It serves to shovel your savings down the drain.

5. Taking Calculated Risks.

5.1. You must protect your savings and investments from loss.

5.2. The first rule of prosperity has never changed: Don't lose money!

5.3. Every emerging man of wealth is always tempted and tested by spurious and dubious planners who do not follow the principle. You must beware of people who know nothing about the truth. They are duty bound to waste your savings.

5.4. The penalty for taking uncalculated risks is always the loss of your savings.

5.5. You will take arms against any temptation to acquire quick wealth. You will study every investment that promises accelerated multiplication of your money. Such investment may, instead, multiply your stress and regrets.

5.6. Everything that grows in nature grows slowly. The growth of your wealth must never be seen as an exception. The best, and the surest way, to grow rich is to grow rich slowly.

5.7. Never take advice about money from him that is not wealthy, honest, or from him who does not have a proof of long standing obedience of the principle. A poor man's advice may heighten your chances of becoming one of his kind.

5.8. The advice of an experienced money manager is always freely given but such advice, innocent as it may look, is equal in money value to the amount you want to invest.

6. Freedom At Home, And At Work

6.1. You will work hard and smart in order to own your own house. This must start with the house where you do your business and then, shift to the house where you reside. This rule is valid only if you are self employed.

6.2. If you run your own business, you must find ways to own the business place long before you proceed to buy your own home. The reverse order shall threaten your working capital and heighten your fear, anxiety and stress.

6.3. Owning your own home grants you confidence.

6.4. Owning your dwelling place permits you the freedom of regular renovations , improvements and luxurious decor as your treasure grows and multiplies.

6.5. Living in reasonable luxury is a great medicine for your soul.

6.6. Living in reasonable luxury grants you the feeling of opulence and abundance. What you feel about, you bring about. You feel confident.

6.7. If you remain as a tenant in another man's house, your family is a second class citizen on the premises. You must not permit this to last too long.

6.8. A tenant must beg for permission, and so must do his family, about their movements and activities within the place of dwelling. I do not intend to mention that the absence of freedom of movement is akin to slavery or apartheid as these words may prove too strong to bear.

6.9. If you own your own house, the money you would regularly cough out as rents would help in mortgage repayments or go to improving the quality of your dwelling place or improving the worth of your investment.

6.10. Presently inexplicable blessings come to him that own his own house.

7. Power Over Fear

7.1. Loss is the greatest source of fear, and fear is the fiercest enemy of prosperity.

7.2. To sustain the confidence that prosperity confers, it's wise to protect your wealth against unforeseen loss. This shall serve to help remove the l a s t t r a c e o f anxiety and fear, and substitute serenity and peace of mind.

7.3. Love is a very powerful positive emotion. Fear, again, is its rabid enemy. Protection of the beloved is the number one priority of the prosperous. To have the feelings that your family will be safe at all times, even after death, will confer tremendous peace to your soul and confidence to your being.

7.4. It's prudent to keep putting away some amount of money called premium with a reputable insurance company against a possible loss of life and prosperity.

7.5. If you live in a country where the insurance is moribund. Your strategy shall manifest creativity. You will seek an alternative and reasonable course of action.

7.6. An alternative arrangement to number five above might be for you to keep large enough money in a reliable bank or credible stock that matches the promise of the insurance company. Your skill of saving will be there, loyal and handy, to aid you in this regard.

7.7. If you desire that your belongings be shared according to your will, following an untimely death, you prepare a will. If you have no legal will, then your beloved would be at the mercy of merciless.

7.8. Keeping large amount of money for family members as a form of insurance or relying on the promise of an insurance company to haul plentiful money at your family, upon untimely death, is both foolish and unreasonable; it reasons itself to absurdity. A swollen purse, however the amount of money it may contain, will soon be empty unless there's constant refill.

7.9. The best insurance you can grant every member of your family is called earning ability. This is consequently the best legacy. Earning ability is the ability to earn. The ability to earn, the skill of earning, like the skill of saving, is dependent on the skill of learning. Earning is learnable. It is teachable.

8. Learning To Learn

8.1. The best ability is called dependability. The most dependable ability is the ability to earn, and to keep earning.

8.2. To earn, you learn. To keep earning, you keep learning. The more you learn, the more you earn.

8.3. To earn, there must be a desire that is strong and definite. To have a general desire to earn is to exhibit weak longings for wealth.

8.4. A general desire to prosper fetches only poor passion.

The enthusiasm is aroused once a specific amount, like two million naira, is wanted very strongly.

8.5. The strength of your desire to earn must be matched by the strength of your desire to learn.

8.6. The desire to earn, to repeat, must be definite. A large sum of money is indefinite. Two million naira is definite. The desire to learn, like the desire to earn, must also be strong and definite.

8.7. A strong desire to learn already explains itself, but for learning to be specific or definite, you will love and learn only what can translate to money. What you put into your head must be transmitted to what you put in your pocket. You will only read books that promise to fetch what you desire.

8.8. If you read a book or attend a seminar that grants you the idea that doubles your income, the value of the book is not the retail price but the amount of money it helps you to get. Similarly, if a book grants you the insight to guide against the loss of ten million naira you would have otherwise invested wrongly, the real value of the book is the ten million naira you have been enabled to rescue from the jaws of ignorance.

8.9. If what you desire is one million naira, then you have a duty to perfect a plan. The plan is nothing more than a list of practical steps you can take in order to get the money.

8.10. Once the money is realized, you keep recycling and upgrading the same steps that generated the original money. You improve on such steps to get progressively higher earnings. This is the way to prosper.

8.11. You really need to work harder on yourself than you do on your job. You expose yourself to books after books. You show up in seminars after seminars that enable you to perfect the skills of your profession. As you do, you increase your confidence; intelligence and competence that ultimately make you climb to the very top and rub shoulders with the top 1% of the highest earners in your industry.

8.12. You must find ways to learn from the best in your profession. You will determine what they do that makes them matriculate to the zenith. You will proceed to do a great job on yourself in order to end up with the kind of results they get. You do what successful people do, even if it is not convenient.

9. Parting Counsel

This shall not attempt, in any way, to summarize the principles. It must be seen as an inseparable component. Let's go.

i. If you are not already neck deep in debt. You must stay out of it.

ii. If you are currently in debt, you must pay your debt very promptly. You dig yourself out of debt as rapidly as you can.

iii. You must never borrow what you carry no established capacity to pay for.

iv. When you need money, think about the way to earn it. Never think about the possibility of borrowing.

v. You must throw away the credit cards if you have no surplus funds in your debit cards.

vi. Always occupy your mind with the idea of a debt free life.

vii. Find ways to think about how your life will look like if you are already wealthy. If you can imagine it, you can feel it, then you can attract it.

viii. You must take care of your family.

ix. You must contribute to charity. Where charity exists, fear always exits. This, you must bear in mind.

Divine prosperity, great health and long life shall be your portion.

www.ingramcontent.com/pod-product-compliance
Lightning Source LLC
Chambersburg PA
CBHW070940210326
41520CB00021B/6983